WALKS FROM YOUR

AMBLESIDE AND GRASMERE
including the LANGDALES

by
Tom Bowker

DALESMAN

1992

Dalesman Publishing Company Ltd.,
Clapham, via Lancaster, LA2 8EB

First published 1983
Third edition 1991
Reprinted 1992

ISBN: 1 85568 015 7

Printed and bound by The Lavenham Press Ltd., Lavenham, Suffolk

Contents

Cover map by Susan Smith

Key to maps

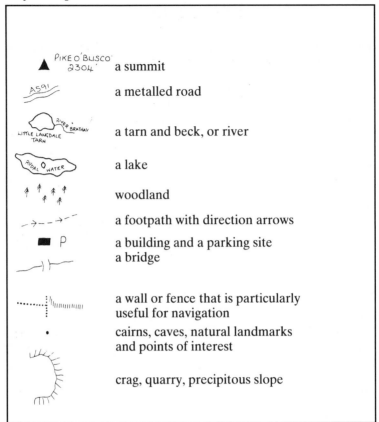

▲ PIKE O'BLISCO 2304'   a summit

A591   a metalled road

LITTLE LANGDALE TARN / RIVER BRATHAY   a tarn and beck, or river

RYDAL WATER   a lake

woodland

a footpath with direction arrows

▪ P   a building and a parking site
a bridge

a wall or fence that is particularly useful for navigation

• cairns, caves, natural landmarks and points of interest

crag, quarry, precipitous slope

Introduction

THIS guidebook is not for the motorist who is looking for a couple of miles stroll in his driving shoes. Nor is it for the hardened long-distance fellwalker. It is written principally for the motorist-cum-walker who is prepared to pull on a pair of boots or stout walking shoes, sling a pack on his/her back and be happy to be out for at least two or three hours. Many of the walks described may also appeal to family parties; to those introducing their children to the hills. For there are many facets to these walks other than the attaining of summits. There are tarns and pools for bathing, woods, waterfalls, lovely picnic spots and caves that would appeal to children. All the walks are circular, starting and finishing at the same point but returning by a different route to that embarked upon in order to add interest. The walks described are divided into three types.

1.   Valley Walks. There are only three genuine circular valley walks in this booklet for the simple reason that they are hard to find. The two main problems are that the nearer to valley level the more problems with access across private or farm land, and that the very nature of Lakeland tends to force the walker uphill eventually. The three described however are good of their type and certainly worth exploring. I generally advise boots or stout walking shoes but given dry conditions the training-type shoe would be perfectly adequate for these particular walks. It must be remembered however that any Lakeland walk will have its boggy patches and that care must be taken on the wet or slimy rocks at the edge of streams or waterfalls.

2.   Medium Walks. These are walks that reach one or more summits over one thousand but below two thousand feet above sea level. They form the bulk of the walks in the booklet for I felt they would appeal most to the kind of motorist-cum-walker-cum-family party described above. They do however cover similar type of ground to the fell-walks of Section 3 and strictly speaking the same rules about clothing and footwear described in that section apply here. Given dry summer conditions however some of these walks could be done in lighter footgear but care must be taken.

3.   Fell Walks. These are walks that reach one or more summits over two thousand feet above sea level. They are not, however, strenuous walks of their type, either being of no great length or over relatively easy ground. Where there is any possibility of the walker getting into difficulty easier alternatives are given. Nevertheless these are fell-walks and should be treated with respect, especially in bad or winter conditions. I do not wish to labour the point but would not rest easy if I did not emunerate here a few basic rules. It is advisable to wear boots, carry a map, compass, whistle and waterproofs. In winter conditions a torch, gloves, balaclava, spare sweater, a plastic survival-bag and spare food are advisable additions. Loose fitting jeans are okay in summer but warmer covering is advisable in winter. Never be afraid to turn back if the weather deteriorates and if you are forced to use your compass start using it at a point where you know where you are, then you have a fixed point to return to - don't wait until you are lost.

All the walks described are accompanied by a rough sketch-map. In clear weather, used sensibly and combined with the text, they should be more than adequate. It is advised, however, particularly for the fell-walks, to also carry the one-inch Ordnance Survey 'Tourist' Map, or the applicable sheet of the Ordnance Survey, 'The English Lakes', 1:25000 Outdoor Leisure Maps. As well as being a better aid to navigation, being more detailed than sketch-maps, they also, particularly the one-inch, help you to identify the various peaks and lakes seen from a particular summit or viewpoint. The mileages are approximate and 'left' or 'right' refers to an object as facing it. A note on car-parking is included with every walk but this situation can be somewhat fluid. In the last booklet I produced for *Dalesman* I also included notes for parking with every walk described. To my horror, almost at the same moment that the book was published, the local authority closed down one of my described car-parks and opened a new one some distance away. So please don't blame the author if a particular parking situation differs from the description, it is as accurate and up-to-date as I can make it.

All the walks described here are on official rights-of-way; or permissive footpaths; or on public access areas. Routes can, however, be legally changed from time to time by developments or road improvements, in which case there should be a signpost specifically indicating the alteration.

When I was first given the opportunity to write this booklet I had some doubts about the project as my interest had always been with the high fells. As the work progressed however I found myself discovering facets of Lakeland that I was unaware existed despite thirty years of walking upon these fells. I became fascinated by hills and footpaths that I must admit I had previously scorned. I only hope that the readers of this booklet discover as much pleasure from these walks as I did. This edition has been extensively revised where I felt it necessary. Should, however, you come across footpath, or signpost, changes I have missed and would be prepared to inform me of the details, via the publisher, you will receive my grateful thanks. Happy walking!

Tom Bowker

LANGDALE

Pike O'Blisco via Oxendale

Though overshadowed by higher and more glamorous neighbours, this surprisingly craggy little fell offers an entertaining traverse and lovely views.

Parking: In the carpark to the right of the Old Dungeon Ghyll Hotel. (GR 286062).

WALK back over the bridge to the road. Turn right and pass through the gate ahead to follow the farm track to Stool End Farm. Behind the farm rises the broad ridge known as The Band. Pass through the farmyard and follow the path climbing alongside a wall. Ignore a path forking right and continue alongside the wall to a stile leading into the valley of Oxendale. Walk up the valley, passing through a narrow gated passage alongside a sheepfold at one point, to where a footbridge on your left spans the Oxendale Beck.

Step on to the bridge but pause on it to read two small memorial plaques fixed to the left-hand handrail. Then turn and look up the dale. Soaring above the dalehead, on a two thousand foot rampart of crag and deeply cut gill, are the 'crinkles' of Crinkle Crags. The shadow-pooled gill driving deep into their stony entrails is Crinkle Gill. A relatively easy 'scramble' it provides an entertaining way on to the summit ridge. The sombre cleft curving over the silvery thread of Whorneyside Force is Hell Gill, a shorter but slightly more serious 'scramble'.

Cross the bridge and climb the renovated path to cross the neck of a ridge, under the summit rocks of Pike O'Blisco, to find yourself overlooking Browney Gill. As you climb, behind you the craggy skyline of the Langdale Pikes rises above the crest of The Band. Browney Gill is the remaining one of Crinkle Crag's triumvirate of 'gill scrambles'. Its lower section is largely a rough walk interspersed with entertaining 'pitches' of 'scrambling'. Its upper section, twisting up into the crags of Great Knott, is best left well alone.

Continue climbing up the fellside above the gill, passing close to the head of a fine waterfall at one point, to eventually emerge on to the broad grassy saddle dividing Pike O'Blisco and Cold Pike. Turn round and look back at one of the finest mountain views in Lakeland.

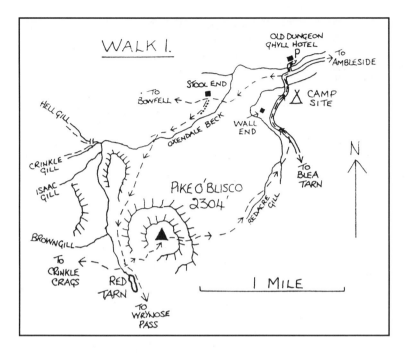

Don't just take my word for it, the great Wainwright chose it as the dust cover for his best-selling "Fellwalking with Wainwright", which must say something about it.

Beyond the saddle lies Red Tarn and beyond that the Coniston Fells rise above the valley of the Wrynose Pass. The cocky cone of Dow Crag is particularly recognisable. If the paths hereabouts are wet you will find your bootsoles sticky with bright red mud. Postlethwaite's classic "Mines and Mining in the English Lake District" states that iron ore was once mined near Red Tarn, which probably accounts for the name of the tarn and the texture of the paths. Climb left up the Pike O'Blisco path and you'll see evidence of a mine shaft that has collapsed in upon itself during recent years. I hope nobody was sitting there eating their "butties' at the time!

Climb past the shaft up the path that twists steadily up to the summit rocks of Pike O'Blisco. It ends in a kind of rocky trench. Climb left over slabby rock to the summit cairn. 'Pike' means 'sharp summit'; 'Blisco' is unexplained and possibly a personal name. Particular points of interest in the view are, south-easterly, Windermere, with the hazy hump of Ingleborough far beyond; and across the airy gulf of Langdale the pallid slash of Stone Axe Gully (described in Walk 2).

To descend, cross the trench and follow a path passing to the left of the cairn-crowned mound of the lower of the fell's twin tops. The path now veers more steeply left down to meet the first of the short rocky scrambles that pass through the belts of rock guarding this side of the fell. None of these 'rock steps' are unduly difficult unless plastered with ice. Should such conditions occur on any, or all, of these 'steps', walk right to find an easier way down the rocks, *not* left.

Beyond the last belt of crag the ground levels out until the path reaches the rim of Redacre Gill. A steep, eroded path descends the left bank before crossing the beck onto an easier-angled path which leads down to the road. Turn left and follow the road back to your car.

The Langdale Pikes
via Dungeon Ghyll

The Langdale Pikes must be known to a high percentage of this country's population. People who have never set foot on a fellside must be familiar with the rugged skyline that has graced untold calendars, Christmas cards and book covers. They were the first mountains I ever climbed, some forty years ago, and undoubtedly many walkers hold them in that same sentimental regard. The walk described below has some mild scrambling in its early stages but if you find yourself deterred by this it can be avoided. This scrambling however leads to two hidden waterfalls and a splendid rocky gorge.

Parking: In the free car-park, on the right, just beyond the entrance drive to the Stickle Barn complex. (GR 295065).

AT the lower end of the car park, above a gate, a path climbs right through the trees to a kissing-gate. Beyond it, turn left to another kissing-gate. Beyond this turn right and follow the wall, passing a seat, to reach another kissing-gate. Beyond this cross the stream and follow the well-worn path on its left bank. After a short climb a path will be seen slanting down to the right into the bed of the ghyll, and the entrance to the rocky shaft containing Dungeon Ghyll Force. Stepping carefully and depending upon the amount of water coming down it is possible to enter the gloomy rift and peer up at the roaring fall. Coleridge, himself an active and enthusiastic fell-walker, is reputed to have modelled the waterfall in his poem 'Kubla Khan' upon this Lakeland cascade. Indeed, in the late forties, a literary minded English rock-climber celebrated both this and his first ascent of a new hard climb on Pavey Ark by christening the climb 'Alph'.

    Climb back out and continue up the path until yet another path slants down into the bed of the ghyll, above the falls. Follow the stream bed, which may entail zig-zagging from bank to bank, until it turns right to meet another fine cascade and a rock pool. Scramble up the left-hand bank of the cascade and follow the stream into a rocky gorge. Follow its fascinating twists for a mile or so. There is some interesting scrambling and again a zig-zag course is necessary. Eventually a lovely high cascade, falling into a rocky basin, is reached. To the left a gully will be seen running into the fellside; scramble up this to reach easy ground. Now follow the stream above the cascade. Loft Crag and Harrison Stickle now tower impressively ahead with the craggy crest of Pavey Ark thrusting up further to the

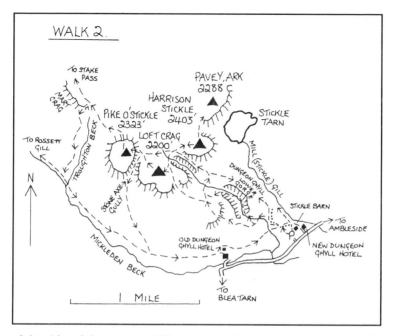

WALK 2.

TO STAKE PASS

MART CRAG

PAVEY, ARK 2288 C

HARRISON STICKLE 2403'

PIKE O'STICKLE 2323'

STICKLE TARN

LOFT CRAG 2200'

TO ROSSETT GILL

TROUGHTON BECK

MILL (STICKLE) GILL

DUNGEON GHYLL UPPER GORGE

DUNGEON GHYLL LOWER GORGE

STICKLE BARN

N

STONE AXE GULLY

TO AMBLESIDE

NEW DUNGEON GHYLL HOTEL

MICKLEDEN BECK

OLD DUNGEON GHYLL HOTEL

1 MILE

TO BLEATARN

right. Ahead the stream will be seen to disappear into another rocky gorge. A way can be made up this but the scrambling involved is more serious and I do not feel I should recommend it in a guide-book of this type.

It is possible that some readers of this booklet may have already been deterred from entering the lower gorge because of the 'scramble' up the left-hand bank of the first cascade. If this happens return downstream and climb back on to the original path. Follow this until the angle eases and Loft Crag and Harrison Stickle can be seen ahead. A walk to the right now should bring you back to the bank of the ghyll, above the high cascade and the gorge. Whichever way you arrive at this point now cross the stream and climb the obvious path on the far (right) bank. Follow this path which becomes more rocky and interesting as it traverses below the steep broken crags of Harrison Stickle and above the upper gorge of the Dungeon Ghyll. Eventually easier ground is reached and a junction with the 'tourist' route. Turn right along this and a short climb brings you to the summit of Harrison Stickle. The view is extensive and particularly fine towards Windermere. There is a fine 'birdseye' view of Stickle Tarn below and an interesting profile of Pavey Ark's climbing crag. To the west the Scafells and the 'hump' of Gable are predominant with the cocky thrust of Pike O'Stickle, your next objective, in the

11

foreground. Return back and cross the stream at the head of the gorge. A well-worn path will be seen heading directly towards Pike O'Stickle. If the day is clear however an interesting alternative which requires little extra expenditure of energy is to first climb the less obtrusive peak of Loft Crag. From it head towards Pike O'Stickle by following the edge of the crags. By looking down to the left a superb view will be seen of the north-west face of Gimmer Crag, where lie some of Lakeland's hardest rock-climbs. The original path is now joined at the foot of the summit rocks of Pike O'Stickle. To your left, at this point, an obvious gully drops steeply away.

This gully is known as Stone Axe Gully due to the discovery, in 1947, that a small square-cut cave in its right wall was a 'factory' for the production of Neolithic axe-heads. Since then other 'factories' have been uncovered on Harrison Stickle, Glaramara, Great End and Scafell Pike. Evidently these Neolithic fellsmen were not only expert field geologists but capable of organising a system of production and distribution that saw Lakeland axe-heads exported to a wide area of the British Isles. The rock architecture on both sides of the gully is splendid and the cave lies about a third of the way down. To be honest, however, the descent is not recommended unless you are experienced in descending loose, shaly gullies that have become badly eroded by the slithery passage of thousands of axe-head seekers. If you have any doubts about your ability to cope with such terrain leave Stone Axe Gully and continue as follows.

Cross the head of the gully and scramble up to the summit of Pike O'Stickle for a breathtaking view of the notched skylines of Bowfell and Crinkle Crags across the airy gulf of Mickleden. Descend the summit rocks and head north-westerly along a path following the rim of the fell. This eventually descends into the hollow at the head of Troughton Beck, which it crosses before swinging sharply left to reach the rim of Mart Crag. From here it descends in steepish zig-zags eventually to join the main Langdale-Rossett Gill track on the floor of Mickleden. Now turn left along this track. When the gate at the rear of the Old Dungeon Ghyll Hotel is approached bear left up the fellside to a higher gate. Pass through this into a walled lane which passes behind a white house standing above the hotel. Follow this lane eventually to cross a footbridge over the Dungeon Ghyll and rejoin your outward route.

Lingmoor and Side Pike
via Blea Tarn

A superb short walk taking in a variety of terrain and scenery and starting and finishing at a lovely picnic spot, with the possible chance of a close-up of rock-climbers in action. An excellent walk for introducing children to the hills with a promise of a paddle or swim in the tarn and a picnic by its shores at the end.

Parking: In the National Trust car-park, near Blea Tarn, on the road connecting Great Langdale with Little Langdale. (GR 296044).

LEAVE the car-park, turn right, and walk up the road. Shortly after the wall on your right turns away look for a faint path slanting up the fellside. Climb this to join a more well-worn path on the right bank of the gill spilling down towards Blea Tarn House. Turn right up this path. Pause at your leisure, for the prospect behind you is worth any excuse for a 'breather'. The Langdale Pikes, towering above the craggy cone of Side Pike, dominate of course. Bowfell, five hundred feet higher and the true king of Langdale's mountains, stands back and you only get a taste of the mighty rampart it forms, with Crinkle Crags, around the dalehead. Below your toe-caps gleams Blea Tarn, a delight yet to come. Beyond the depths of Little Langdale rise Wetherlam, Swirl How, and Great Carrs, northern outliers of the Coniston Fells.

Eventually your path moves left, through some splendid pines, into the head of the gill to a stile. Cross the stile and turn left to climb steeply alongside the wall/fence to shortly reach a stile in a fence leading to the large cairn crowning aptly named Lingmoor, 'the fell of the heather, or ling'. The 2½" map says 'Brown Howe' but Wainwright, Griffin, a million fellwalkers, and me, call it 'Lingmoor'. Windermere is now added to the view and for the collector of scenic curiosities, given a clear day, Blackpool Tower may be picked out to the left of Wetherlam (the furthest left of the Coniston Fells).

Descend beyond the cairn following the path alongside the wall/ fence crowning the fell, the Langdale Pikes looking more magnificent with every onward step. Below, to your right, lies unpublicised and rarely visited Lingmoor Tarn. Yet I have seen its surface sown with the lovely Bogbean, and the Pikes, blazoned in Autumn colours, mirrored pin-sharp there. After a rocky step, awkward when slimy or icy, a stile transfers you across the fence/wall. Now follow the wall towards the increasingly forbidding crags of Side Pike. Don't worry,

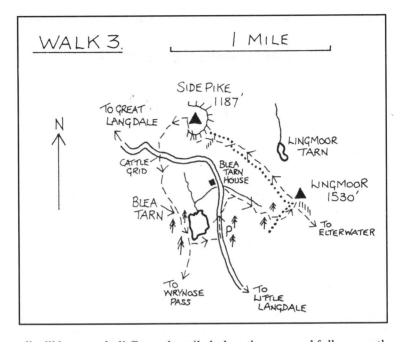

WALK 3.   1 MILE

SIDE PIKE 1187'
TO GREAT LANGDALE
LINGMOOR TARN
CATTLE GRID
BLEA TARN HOUSE
LINGMOOR 1530'
BLEA TARN
TO ELTERWATER
P
TO WRYNOSE PASS
TO LITTLE LANGDALE
N

all will be revealed! Cross the stile below the crag and follow a path which climbs right, then left, then down and round to a ledge apparently blocked by a rock pinnacle. Pushing your rucksack before you squeeze behind the pinnacle onto the ledge beyond. It's good fun and much easier than it looks. I've encouraged several dubious and 'pleasantly plump' ladies and gentlemen safely through. Ancient climbing guidebooks used to call such features a 'Fat Man's Agony'. Follow the ledge around a corner and climb a path forking right to eventually meet an old wall and more worn path. Turn right and follow this to reach the summit of Side Pike. The Pikes look even more impressive from here. Retrace your steps and follow the path alongside the wall down to a stone memorial bench and a stile leading onto the road.

Cross the road, go left through a gap in a wall and down towards Blea Tarn. A tunnel of rhododendrons leads you along the western shore then turn left over a footbridge onto the open, grassy south shore. Pause here and look with pride at the rugged skyline you have traversed, and the real and water-mirrored array of Pike O'Stickle, Loft Crag, Harrison Stickle, and Pavey Ark. (Julie Walters and friends 'skinny-dipped' here in the film 'She'll Be Wearing Pink Pyjamas'). Your car is nearby so you have time to follow suit!

The Langdale Valley

A pleasant amiable walk that is nowhere strenuous. Ideal for children or 'potterers' who wish to picnic, sketch, bird-watch, flower-watch, or whatever. There is a variety of scenery from open river-bank to thick woodland. Craggy ridges rise on both sides and dominating all is perhaps the finest view of the Langdale Pikes at their classical best.

Parking: The National Trust car-park in Elterwater village, opposite the Brittania Inn. If this is full park on Elterwater Common.

LEAVE the car-park and turn left. Cross the bridge over the Great Langdale Beck and turn immediately right up a tarmac drive, signposted 'Public Footpath'. Climb between large boulders to fork right, at a 'Footpath' sign, on to a stony path leading down towards the beck. The buildings across the beck, now a time-share complex, stand on the site of a former gunpowder mill that was opened in 1824 and in production until the 1930's. The production of 'black powder' was a hazardous process and it has been estimated that up to fifty workers were killed in accidents in Lakeland's once thriving gunpowder mills.

A faint path forking right through a gap in a wall leads to the edge of a waterslide. Scramble around a rocky hummock and along the slaty rim of the beck to rejoin the stony path through a gap in a wall. Turn right to shortly cross the beck by a footbridge and emerge on to the B5343. Turn left, past the Wainwrights Inn (no, not the guidebook writer), and follow the road round to the right to shortly see a 'Public Footpath' sign on your left. Follow it into a walled lane behind the school. At a junction with a tarmac strip turn left to pass white-painted Thrang Farm. Go through a gate marked 'The Thrang' and pass to the right of the building beyond into a narrow walled lane. 'Thrang' means 'a narrow passage'. At a path junction bear left to re-cross the Great Langdale Beck by a stone bridge. Notice the inscription in the left-hand parapet 'Built 1818. John and Jane Atkinson'.(Aeons ago, whilst camping at Bays Brown Farm, we swam in the fine pool under the bridge).

Cross the bridge and follow the path alongside the beck. Across the meadows to your left are the buildings of Bays Brown Farm, and towering above them the craggy, quarried flank of Lingmoor, 'the fell of the ling, or heather'. Continue pleasantly alongside the beck, through gates or over stiles, with the gill-cleft, crag-pimpled Langdale Pikes rising majestically ahead. At a gate the path veers left, alongside

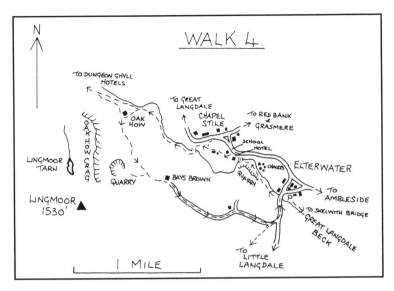

N

WALK 4.

TO DUNGEON GHYLL HOTELS

TO GREAT LANGDALE

CHAPEL STILE

TO RED BANK & GRASMERE

OAK HOW

OAK HOW CRAG

SCHOOL HOTEL

LINGMOOR TARN

ELTERWATER

QUARRY

BAYS BROWN

QUARRY

LINGMOOR 1530'

TO AMBLESIDE

P

TO SKELWITH BRIDGE

GREAT LANGDALE BECK

TO LITTLE LANGDALE

1 MILE

a fence, cutting across a bend in the beck. Beyond the next gate follow the path bearing left towards the buildings of Oak How Farm. Pass in front of the farmhouse to where a 'Public Footpath' sign points right, above a blue waymarker arrow pointing straight ahead. Follow the arrow, passing to the right of a yew tree. Cross a beck and pass between crumbling walls before turning left and climbing up to a gate. If you examine the crags above you may be able to pick out the Oak How Needle, a semi-detached obelisk that attracts rock-climbers. The path shortly passes through mixed woodland. (I have spotted red squirrels in these woods). Squirrels have a long history in Lakeland lore. They have been depicted on a runic stone found at Bewcastle; on thirteenth-century glass in Bowness; and everyone's heard of Squirrel Nutkin. When the path joins the rough road leading to Spout Crag Quarry turn left and down through the yard of Bays Brown Farm onto the tarmac road. Roughly translated, 'Bays Brown' means 'Bruni's Cowshed' and it's reputedly the site of one of the earliest homesteads in Langdale. Note the slate facing on the front of the farmhouse.

Continue along the road, ignoring the 'Permissive Footpath to Chapel Stile', and shortly climb through woods. A small tarn will be seen down through the trees on your left. A faint path leads down to a grassy knoll in the trees overlooking it. I've sat quietly here watching a heron fishing in the tarn. Return to the road and follow it past a house. Ignore the 'Public Bridleway' signs beyond and continue with the tarmac until you join the Elterwater-Little Langdale road. Turn left down into Elterwater.

Walk 5   **Valley Walk, 5½ miles**

The Elterwater Round

A fine all-weather walk full of interest. It holds two rivers, two fine waterfalls, a unique slate gallery, a minor lake, a huge man-made cavern, and numerous picnic and bathing places in its few miles.

Parking: The National Trust car-park in Elterwater village, opposite the Brittania Inn.

GO through the gate signposted 'Riverside Walk to Skelwith Bridge'. The path follows the river-bank then enters the wood bordering Elterwater, 'the swan lake'. Beyond the woods it emerges into open fields again before reaching a gate leading into the gorge containing Skelwith Force. 'Skelwith', roughly translated, means 'the noisy water near a wood, or ford'. The cascade is a fine one, particularly in spate, and bridges lead out onto the rocks for a closer look. After inspecting the falls continue along the river bank, passing through the buildings of the slateworks, to reach Kirkstone Slate Galleries, which are open seven days a week.

After visiting the galleries walk down the drive to Skelwith Bridge. Cross the bridge and follow the road round the sharp corner and up the hill to reach a signpost indicating 'Colwith Bridge', to the right. Turn into the access lane where, after a short walk, a gate signposted 'Colwith Bridge' will be seen on the left. Beyond this the path climbs over a wooded hill to meet a grassy drive coming in from the road on the left. From this point Wetherlam can be seen rising to the left of the trees ahead whilst to their right can be seen Pike O'Blisco and the triple-peaked Crinkle Crags. Turn right along the drive and follow it down past a farmhouse. Ahead, across a field, will be seen a row of caravans. Follow the path heading towards these, looking to the right for a distant view of Seat Sandal and Fairfield, with Dollywaggon Pike filling the gap of Grisedale Hause between them.

Pass through a gate and climb up past the caravans to reach a signpost indicating 'Colwith'' is to the left. Walk through a farmyard to where 'public footpath' is indicated in a gap between two buildings. Beyond the gap head down across the grass; there is a sign 'Colwith' in the hedge to your right. A stile is now reached from which a fine view of the Langdale Pikes can be seen. The path now leads down to a stile in the end of a wall. Beyond this a narrow passage leads on to a drive on to the other side of which is a kissing-gate. Pass through the gate and follow the path down the field to a stile at the edge of a wood. Beyond this the path runs high above the river before dropping down

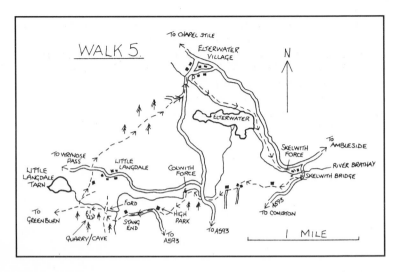

to the water's edge and yet another stile. Now cross over a field to a stile leading on to a road. Turn right along the road but before reaching the bridge (Colwith Bridge), a stile will be seen on the left, signposted 'Public Footpath'. Beyond the stile the path forks. Take the lower right fork, alongside the river, to eventually reach a rocky point overlooking Colwith Force, to my mind the superior of the two waterfalls. 'Colwith' means the 'charcoal wood'.

To continue, follow the path leading above the falls and along the river to reach a stile. Beyond this the path begins to climb up through the woods, passing one particularly fine beech tree, to reach a gate. Pass through this and walk alongside a wall to reach another gate from where there is a superb view of Bowfell framed between Pike O'Blisco and Lingmoor. Pass through this gate to reach High Park Farm and through the farmyard to reach a road. Now turn right down the road to reach the cottages at Stang End.

Continue down the road which crosses a bridge over a beck before swinging around a wooded hill to a ford and footbridge over the River Brathay. Walk left, past the footbridge, following the path above and alongside the river. Keep your eyes open for a gate on your left beyond which a path climbs through a slate spoil-heap. Go through the gate, climb left, then right, to a hut with a National Trust emblem on its door.

Behind the hut is a rock fissure crowned by a slate arch. Pass under the arch and follow the fissure, do not be deterred by the low wet tunnel ahead, and continue until a hidden opening on the left leads to a dramatic view of a huge man-made cavern supported by a central

18

leaning pillar. **(Since writing this account I have visited this spot to find there has been a heavy rockfall into the fissure, and in order to view the cavern you have to climb over the fall. The cavern is a magnificent sight but obviously there is some danger and it is up to each individual to decide if the risk is warranted).**

Return down through the gate then walk left to where a kissing-gate in the wall on your right leads down to the lovely packhorse Slaters Bridge. This is a lovely spot for a picnic and there are fine bathing pools above and below the bridge. Cross the bridge and follow the path running up alongside the wall to reach a gate leading into a lane. There is a fine view back across Little Langdale Tarn towards Wetherlam, Great Carrs, and the twisting road leading up to Wrynose Pass. Turn left along the lane to meet the road. Go left along this a little way before turning right up a lane marked 'Unfit for Cars'. After some climbing the lane eventually descends through woods to meet a road. Turn left down this and soon Elterwater village is entered near to the car-park.

AMBLESIDE

Walk 6   **Fell Walk, 7 miles**

Red Screes via Scandale

An excellent fell-walk of its type. Nowhere really strenuous and giving a superb variety of scenery.

Parking: In one of Ambleside's car-parks.

WALK up the street (North Road) behind the shops facing the Bus Station and Gaynors shop, to its junction with Smithy Brow, above the Golden Rule pub. Climb right to shortly see a 'High Sweden Bridge Lane' sign on your left. Climb left up this lane, ignoring a left fork 'Low Sweden Bridge', to where the tarmac ends at a gate. Beyond the gate the lane narrows, between drystone walls, and becomes rough underfoot. Already there is a fine view over the left-hand wall, down into the Rothay valley and across to Loughrigg and beyond it to the Langdale and Coniston fells. The lane twists and climbs steadily through woods before eventually emerging into the high valley of Scandale. The path forks here with the left-hand path crossing Scandale Beck by a packhorse bridge (High Sweden Bridge), before climbing up to the crest of the Low Pike to High Pike ridge. This ridge is the tip of the right-hand horn of the popular Fairfield Horseshoe walk.

Your way lies straight ahead, however, up Scandale - 'the short dale'. Red Screes is the rounded fell to the right and the saddle straight ahead is Scandale Pass, with the twin-peaks of Little Hart Crag peering cockily over it. A 'green' road can be seen running directly up the floor of the U-shaped valley to end a few hundred feet below the crest of the pass. It is not, as it might appear, a drove road but a kind of funnel built in order to move sheep quickly down the fells. Many of Lakeland's myriad walls were built in the period 1795-1820. A growing population created a demand for food and the successive wars with France doubled the price of wool. Both these causes led to an increase in the enclosure of formerly barren land. The history of Lakeland wall-building must be worth a treatise in itself. Many walls go back long before the period mentioned. A collapsed dike on Nab Scar, above Rydal, can be date 1277. A sheep boundary in Ling Cove, Eskdale, can be dated 1290, and a wall on Red Screes, above Kirkstone Pass, can be dated 1680. Many can be almost regarded as works of art. The wall running along the Low Pike - Dove Crag ridge, above to your left, is continuous for two miles.

The 'funnel' gives pleasant walking and when it ends a good path leads, a little more steeply, up to a stile in the wall running across the crest of Scandale Pass. The valley beyond is called Caiston Glen and the path continues down this and eventually arrives at Patterdale. The steep scree-covered slopes of John Bell's Banner can be seen, above the Kirkstone road, and beyond that the more distant High Street range. To the left is the fine profile of the previously mentioned Little Hart Crag. This is a fine rocky peak apparently rarely climbed. For those with energy to spare it is worth the detour. Simply follow the wall until it veers left, then leave it and head for the base of the rocks. There is a good view from the summit of Dovedale and Brotherswater.

Returning to Scandale Hause, or if you have not left it, attack Red Screes by following the path running alongside the wall. After crossing a mossy slab the angle steepens a little before a bisecting wall is met. Looking down to the left from this section there is a fine view of Brotherswater. Leave the walls now and head easterly, across gradually easing grass slopes, to reach the trig point near a shallow tarn. The trig point is perched on the edge of steep screes and shattered crags giving a bird's-eye view down to Brotherswater. The all-round view is extensive and varied and happy moments could be spent identifying the various fells and lakes.

For the descent head south-westerly, following the path that runs above the eastern edge of the fell. This shortly brings you above the corrie whose sanguine crags and screes give the mountain its name. (On some maps the mountain is called 'Kilnshaw Chimney' but this is actually a natural rock-feature in the crags above Kirkstone). From here a superb bird's-eye view of the Kirkstone Pass Inn and the road junction is seen. The descent is easy, with island-studded Windermere always before your eyes. Eventually a stile over a wall leads into another 'funnel' which twists down to a gate leading out on to the road above 'The Struggle'. Turn right here and Ambleside is shortly reached.

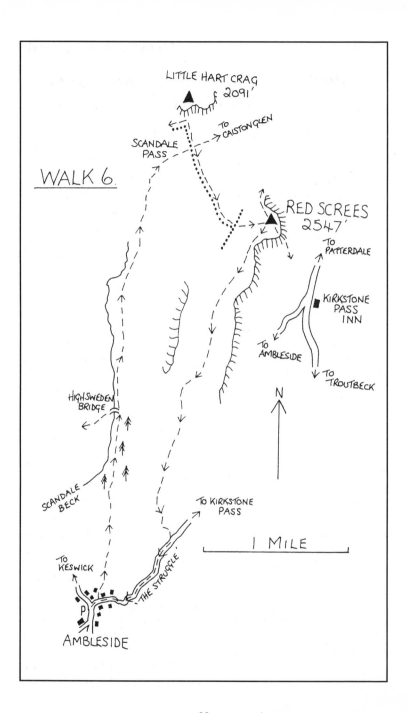

LITTLE HART CRAG 2091'

TO CAISTONGLEN

SCANDALE PASS

WALK 6.

RED SCREES 2547'

TO PATTERDALE

KIRKSTONE PASS INN

TO AMBLESIDE

TO TROUTBECK

N

HIGHSWEDEN BRIDGE

SCANDALE BECK

TO KIRKSTONE PASS

1 MILE

TO KESWICK

THE STRUGGLE

P

AMBLESIDE

Stock Ghyll and The Green Lanes
of Wansfell

This walk is full of variety. The climb up Wansfell requires 'a bit of puff' but the views give ample excuse to pause for a breather and are even finer from the summit. The 'green lanes' are a delight. A walk along them evokes a past Lakeland and it is not hard to imagine a jingling pack-horse train, a pair of moleskin-clad itinerant quarrymen, or a stovepipe-hatted poet and his crinolined entourage, around the next corner. All this plus some fine cascades, a 16th century house of historic interest and a constantly changing variety of scenery makes six-plus miles seem a delightful stroll.

Parking: As for Walk 6.

IN AMBLESIDE, pass between the Market Hall (now a restaurant) and a bank and turn left to follow the lane leading behind the *Salutation Hotel.* Shortly, fork left through a gate into Stock Gill Park. The wooded cascades of Stock Gill Force are worth the diversion, especially if in spate. Paths climb up either bank and there are various viewing points. Just below the head of the falls, in a wall to your right, there is a rusty turnstile. After exploring the falls pass through this on to the lane beyond. This turnstile is a relic of the days when the cascades were privately owned and could only be visited upon payment of a fee. It also vividly recalls to me a school-trip to the Lakes aeons ago.

Turn left to cross over a cattlegrid. From here Red Screes dominates the skyline with the sanguine rocks of the huge corrie below the summit giving vivid testimony to the aptness of its name. A few hundred yards beyond the cattle-grid, near a green hut, a stile in the wall on the right is signposted 'Wansfell' and 'Troutbeck'. Cross the stile and ascend the well-worn path climbing steeply up to the obvious rocky knoll on the skyline above. It's a strenuous climb but as stated the views behind your back give every excuse for a halt. The Rothay valley twists away below your feet, guarded on the right by Fairfield and its satellite peaks and on the left by the hummocky plateau of Loughrigg, whilst beyond Loughrigg there is a dramatic skyline stretching from Coniston Old Man to Ullscarf. Rydal Water graces the head of the valley with just a glint of Grasmere peering around the foot of Nab Scar.

The rocky knoll is not the true summit, which lies a few yards beyond over a stile. The few steps to the top bring a sudden and

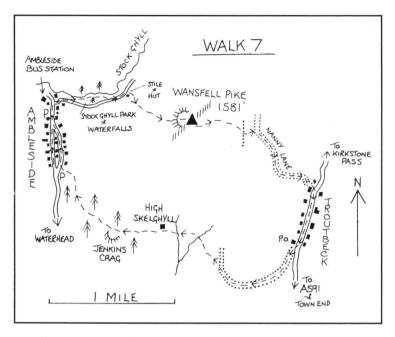

superb view down the gleaming length of Windermere. In the opposite direction the notch of Kirkstone Pass is obvious with the volcano-like summit of Angle Tarn Pike, above Patterdale, peeking over it. Working right from the pass are John Bell's Banner, Thornthwaite Crag, with its splendid chimney-like cairn, followed by the shapely cones of Froswick and Ill Bell, and the the more prosaic Yoke which leads down to the Garburn Pass. Harter Fell (Mardale) can be glimpsed between Thornthwaite Crag and Froswick and also, if the light is right, the spirals of the Roman military road can be seen descending from this same dip. Without an early form of it, apparently 'Wansfell' cannot be interpreted except that the first element may be a personal name.

Descend easterly, along a cairned path, over easy ground, to a gate in a wall. Shortly beyond this another gate leads into Nanny Lane. Turn right and follow this lane which goes most pleasantly down to the village of Troutbeck. Across the other side of the valley the walled lane that leads up to Garburn Pass can be seen slanting across the fellside. Below it is the very popular Lime Fitts Caravan and Camping Site. Upon reaching the road turn right and walk through the village until, just beyond a post-box in a wall, another walled lane forks upwards to the right, signposted 'Bridleway to Ambleside'. (Town End, a 16th century Lakeland dwelling house now owned by the National Trust, lies a short detour down the road should you wish to visit it).

Climb the walled Cock Robin Lane, which gradually levels and swings right. It's delightful walking, above a gleaming Windermere and with Wetherlam, Harrison Stickle, and their like, crowding into view around every corner. A final corner brings Wansfell Pike looming above. A gate/stile signposted 'Ambleside/Jenkin Crag', to your left, leads you gradually down, across a beck and past a ruin, to a tarmac road. Turn right up the tarmac to High Skelghyll Farm. Pass through the yard, and in front of the farmhouse, to a gate leading on to a path descending into Skelghyll Wood. Shortly after entering the wood a sign 'Jenkin Crag' will be seen on your left. Walk out on to its rocky summit for a lovely prospect over Windermere and the humped and lovely fells encircling it. Return to the path and twist down through the woods. (We've spotted a fox hereabouts so keep your eyes open). The path leads onto a tarmac strip which leads down to a road behind a car-park. Cross the car-park to reach Lake Road and follow it back into Ambleside.

Todd Crag and Rydal Park

For me this walk is worth any effort involved simply for the bird's-eye view of the remains of the Roman fort at Waterhead. If however history is not your bent the views are, naturally in Lakeland, superb. There are literary associations and Rydal Cave is impressive; and after the initial climb is achieved the expenditure of energy required is slight.

Parking: As for Walk 6.

LEAVE Ambleside by Compston Road (behind the Bus Station). A few hundred yards down this road turn right into Vicarage Road, signposted 'Rydal Park/Loughrigg'. Walk through Rydal Park and cross the River Rothay by a hump-backed bridge to join a road. Turn right, across a cattle grid, then almost immediately left, across another cattle grid, on to a tarmac bridleway signposted 'Loughrigg'. Climb this until at a sharp right turn, above the buildings at 'Brow Head', a metal stile signposted 'Clappersgate' will be seen on your left. Cross this and walk left to pass through a gap in a slate fence. Paths climb to the right and left of the wooded hillock above you. Climb the left-hand path, heading towards a rocky summit. Cross its cairned top through a gap in a wall. Cross the next summit by a stile over a wall, then a third summit to reach the rocky rounded fourth, and arguably highest, summit of Todd Crag.

The 'birds-eye' view over Windermere is breathtaking. My eyes always wander, however, to the ruins of 'Galava', the Roman fort, on its promontory by the mouth of the Rothay. You're gazing upon the archetypal plan of a military fort that remained unchanged for centuries and was planted upon conquered soil from Persia to Perthshire. Roman sentries may have looked up and seen a Brigante war-party poised, like Apaches in a John Wayne film, on the very rocks upon which you are standing.

Return into the dip between the last two summits and turn down left. Climb over a rise and past a small tarn. Climb again to pass to the right of larger Lily Tarn. Shortly, the path veers left to pass alongside a wall then down to a gate in a fence. Beyond this, cross a path and climb straight over the hillock ahead into a dip with a tiny tarn to your left. Look down to your right to spot a wall. Head for the curving wall corner, crossing en-route a path issuing from a gate. (Should you wish to return directly to Ambleside follow this path through the gate). Near the wall corner stepping stones cross a boggy patch. Just beyond, the path crosses rocks. Fork left here up a path leading to

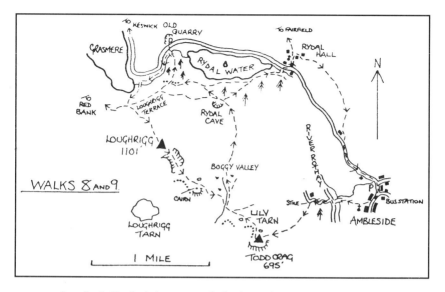

another fork. Fork right now and climb gradually to reach a cairn. Go beyond the cairn and down to eventually pass through an area of dwarf juniper. Dwarf juniper was particularly used for the production of charcoal for Lakeland's now-defunct gunpowder industry. Soon Rydal Water will be seen below with Helm Crag towering impressively beyond. Look over your left shoulder to spot a fine waterfall.

Your path emerges on to a rough track near a beck. (If you have not already visited Rydal Cave (described in Walk 9), climb left up the track, past a quarry/cave guarded by a rock pinnacle, to reach it. After exploring the cave return down the track). If you already have visited Rydal Cave then turn right down the rough track keeping your eyes open for a path dropping down the steep bank on your left, past a seat, to a metal gate in a wall above the lake. Go through this gate and follow a wooded path to a footbridge over the Rothay. (I've seen an otter hereabouts). Cross the bridge and climb up on to the A591. Turn right, then shortly left up the lane leading to Rydal Mount. Look for a 'Public Footpath' sign on your right, above the upper entrance to Rydal Hall. You might find the 'Tea Shop' sign below it more stimulating! Follow the signs between the buildings and over a bridge spanning the Rydal Beck. After passing the last building on your right, turn right and descend steps for a look at a splendid waterfall. Climb back and follow the fenced path through the grounds of Rydal Hall. Etched on the skyline to your right are the heights you have just 'bagged'. Ornamental gates lead onto the A591 and back to Ambleside.

RYDAL

Loughrigg, from Rydal

*From the car-park this modest hill presents a remarkably rugged
character. The ascent, as described, is straightforward but at one point
fairly strenuous, but the view is worth the effort. The descent is not to
be undertaken lightly if thick mist prevails. This side of the hill is an
extensive plateau covered with a network of apparently aimless paths
which twist and turn around seemingly identical brackeny hillocks.
Given clear skies however it adds interest to the walk and a visit to
Rydal Cave is a fine climax.*

*Parking: In the National Trust car-park, through a log archway, in the
derelict quarry below White Moss Common, on the northern verge of
the A591. (GR 348065).*

CROSS the A591 and follow the path down on to the banks of the
Rothay. Turn right, and ignoring the bridge over the river, pass
through a gate. Follow the path alongside the river to a gate. Beyond
it, paths fork. Take the left fork over a rise and down to a footbridge
over the river. Cross the bridge and turn right on to the pebbly beach
which offers a fine prospect of Grasmere and its enfolding fells. The
centre-piece is Helm Crag (The Lion and The Lamb). Rising to its
left is the knobbly ridge of Walk 14, with Ullscarf rising behind it.
Behind Helm Crag rises Steel Fell, with the gap of Dunmail Raise to
its right, this in turn being overshadowed by the curving bulk of Seat
Sandal.

The beach is a lovely spot for a picnic or swim and on a boiling day,
faced by Loughrigg, which rears steeply up behind the beach, you
may decide to cut your losses. Walk to the far end of the beach then
climb steeply left up a rough path between a wall and a beck, to
eventually emerge onto Loughrigg Terrace near a gate. Turn left,
crossing the beck, then shortly fork right up a steepish path. A steady
pull brings a cairned top, which unfortunately proves to be a false
summit. The angle eases now, however, and the trig-point can be
seen crowning the ridge ahead. Stepping up to the trig-point brings
an exhilarating view down the upper reaches of Windermere, with
Esthwaite Water gleaming more discreetly away to its right. The
Langdale Pikes dominate the western skyline, with higher, but more
retiring, Bowfell and Crinkle Crags to their left. Further left, the
great whaleback of Wetherlam superimposes itself upon the Coniston

Fells, with Coniston Old Man peeping over its right shoulder. 'Loughrigg' means 'the ridge above the lake'.

Follow a worn path towards Windermere which drops into a deep hollow between scree slopes. A well-cairned grassy path leads out of the hollow and the view opens up again to your right. Shortly, look for a wall climbing up on to a hummock to your right. Climb on to this hummock, which is crowned by a fine cairn and gives a lovely prospect of Langdale, and, immediately below, Loughrigg Tarn. Descend into the hollow beyond, which has two small tarns to its left. Climb to the right of a hummock on a good path which swings left to a cairn. Twist down towards a shallow boggy valley filled with a meandering beck. When you reach the head of a steep rocky groove in the path pause and examine the ground on the far side of the beck. Two paths march left through the bracken, yours is the upper one. Descend the groove, cross the beck, and climb to where your path forks left, below a split boulder on the skyline. Climb gently to a cairn on a rise. Go beyond the cairn and down to pass eventually through an area of dwarf juniper. Dwarf juniper was particularly used for the production of charcoal for Lakeland's now-defunct gunpowder industry. Soon Rydal Water will be seen below with Helm Crag towering impressively beyond. Look over your left shoulder to spot a fine waterfall.

Your path emerges onto a rough track near a beck. Climb left up this track to pass a damp, derelict quarry/cave guarded by a rock pinnacle. Climb a little further to reach the huge derelict quarry/cave known as Rydal Cave, which is guarded by a pool of crystal clear water. Looking out, the jagged arch of the cave mouth curving over pool, larches, birches, far fellside, and reflections thereof, forms a dramatic composition irresistible to photographers. Though you will probably be dissatisfied with your results, try it, we all do every time we visit! Come out of the cave and turn left to reach a wooden bench just below the cave. Go down a grassy path to a broad track alongside a wall. Turn left along this and a short climb brings you to a gate in the wall leading into a wood. Go down through the wood to cross a footbridge over the Rothay and rejoin your outward route.

Walk 10 Valley Walk, 3½ miles

The Round of Rydal

This delightful and amiable walk can be accomplished in a couple of hours but wisely you will linger over it. You can then appreciate the literary associations, the scenery, and the countless opportunities this walk gives to picnic, swim, paddle, bird-watch, sketch, or whatever takes your fancy.

Parking: As for Walk 9.

FOLLOW The directions for Walk 9 as far as Loughrigg Terrace. Turn left and walk along the Terrace enjoying the fine views it offers. Take the path forking right at the far end of the terrace which traverses across the fellside to reach a wooden bench. Climb above the bench to Rydal Cave (described in Walk 9). After exploring the cave follow the track down past another quarry/cave guarded by a rock pinnacle. Continue down the track looking for a path descending the steep bank to your left, past a seat, to a metal gate in a wall near the lake edge. Go through the gate and follow a wooded path to reach a footbridge over the Rothay just below where it empties from Rydal Water. After crossing the bridge a short climb brings you out on to the A591. Turn right here and follow the road until opposite the lane leading up to Rydal Mount.

Walk up the lane until Rydal Church is seen to your left. Wordsworth worshipped here, indeed he had a hand in choosing the site, and apparently often vociferously disparaged a sermon from the vantage-point of his front pew. If the daffodils are in bloom go through the churchyard into the little wood beyond. This is 'Dora's Field'. The flowers here were planted by the poet in memory of his daughter. After visiting the church continue up the lane to reach Rydal Mount. This was the poet's home for the last period of his life and he died here in 1850. The house is open to the public.

After visiting, or not, continue steeply on to where a narrow lane, signposted 'Public Bridleway/Grasmere', forks left above Rydal Mount. Go through a gate and follow the path which twists and undulates across the wooded south flank of Nab Scar. The trees part periodically, giving lovely views of Rydal Water. 'The dale where rye was grown' is the interpretation of 'Rydal'. Eventually, near a small reedy tarn, the end of a tarmac road is reached. Wordsworth is reputed to have skated on the frozen waters of this tarn. We once disturbed a heron fishing here, and have seen deer on the fellside opposite. Turn left here down a stony path to reach the carpark.

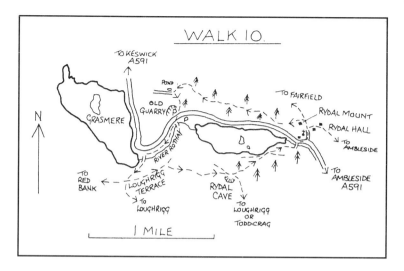

If you have energy to spare, before turning down the stony path, climb the fellside opposite the tarn on to the summit of White Moss Common for a lovely view over Rydal Water and Grasmere.

GRASMERE

Walk 11   **Medium Walk, 3½ miles**

Allcock Tarn

*A pleasant walk combining scenic beauty with literary associations.
This is a good walk for children. I always found the promise of a picnic
near water a remarkable incentive to my children.*

Parking: Grasmere village car-parks.

LEAVE Grasmere village by the road heading towards Ambleside.
Upon reaching the junction with the main-road (Keswick to Ambleside
A591), cross this and follow the minor road leading to Wordsworth's
Dove Cottage. Addicts of the Wordsworth family saga may be tempted
here to visit and inspect some recently discovered letters of the poet.
After a short climb the road forks, signposted 'Rydal' to the right, and
'No Through Road For Motor Vehicles' to the left. Take the left-hand
fork and after another short climb, near a seat, a path signposted
'Footpath To Allcock Tarn' will be seen bearing left. Follow this to a
gate where the path forks. Ignore the path branching up to the right,
alongside the wall, and go through the gate. The path now climbs up
through a tunnel of trees before emerging on to more open ground.

There is a bird's-eye view here down on to Grasmere, lake and
village. Across the valley Helm Crag (The Lion and The Lamb) is
predominant and beyond it Far Easedale leads up to the saddle of
Greenup Edge, with High Raise and Ullscarf rising to the left and right
of this. To the left of High Raise, the Langdale Pikes, Bowfell, Crinkle
Crags, Pike O'Blisco and the Coniston Fells all reveal more of themselves
as height is gained. To the right of Helm Crag bulky Steel Fell stands
guard over the A591 and Dunmail Raise. The path now winds pleasantly
upwards passing a little fish-pond overhung by larch trees. Eventually
the path forks, the right fork leading up to an iron-gate in a walled lane,
whilst the left fork slants through bracken towards a stand of trees.
Climb the left fork, pass through a gate in a wall, and climb steeply up
through a stand of trees. Move left across a beck before climbing
steeply again to reach the rocky summit of Grey Crag. Sunk amongst
these rocks you will see a metal tube. On Grasmere Sports day a flag
is planted here and runners in the Fell Race toil up the steep fellside
below you, round the flag and plunge recklessly downhill.

A short walk beyond leads to a gap in a wall and the banks of Allcock
Tarn. The grassy banks of this lovely but somewhat austere tarn make
a delightful picnic spot. Above the tarn rise the rock-strewn slopes of

Heron Pike. Windermere can be seen to the south, with Morecambe Bay beyond if it is particularly clear, whilst to the west all the fells previously mentioned are spread in finer detail.

To descend follow the path along the edge of the tarn towards a rocky gap. A National Trust sign is reached, near a metal stile. Beyond the stile the path passes through a gap before beginning to swing left and downwards. The valley below is Greenhead Gill, the scene of Wordsworth's 'Michael', and there is an impressive view to the right up the upper reaches of it, dominated by the rounded summit of Great Rigg.

The zig-zag path drops steeply down into the bed of the gill. A bridge-like structure across the stream carries the Thirlmere-Manchester pipeline. The descent ends at a footbridge; cross it then turn left through a gate into a narrow lane. Follow this down to a minor road. A turn left here soon brings you down to the A591 near the *Swan Hotel*. Cross this to the road opposite which leads back into Grasmere village.

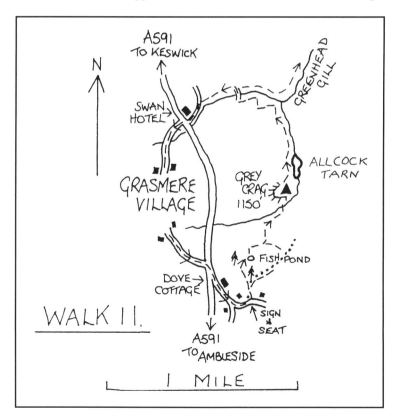

Silver Howe and Lang Howe

*Looking across Grasmere from the A591 or up from Grasmere
village, Silver Howe dominates. Its apparent isolation and mountainous
outline make it appear much higher than its modest height of around
twelve hundred feet. The combined ascent of these two modest fells
nevertheless gives superb views and has a high mountain air about it.*

Parking: As for Walk 11, in Grasmere village.

LEAVE the village by the lane to the left of W. Heaton-Cooper's
studio (there is a coffee-shop on the corner). Follow the lane up the
hill and between two gate-posts near a sign indicating 'Private Road/
Public Footpath'. The house ahead is Allan Bank, yet another
Wordsworth domicile. Those who watched the television drama
based on the life of Wordsworth and directed by Ken Russell may
recognise the exterior. Just below the house the drive forks. A
narrower drive bears right and a small sign indicates 'Path' that way.
This drive steepens and gradually swings to the left. To your right
there is a fine view of Helm Crag, Dunmail Raise and Seat Sandal.
Just before reaching a white house a small sign indicates 'Silver
Howe' to the left. Pass through a gate and follow the path up into a
sunken lane. This leads up to a stile and beyond it to the open fell. The
path now steepens, with a wall to its left. When the wall falls back the
angle eases and the path winds through stunted juniper bushes to
reach two cairns. Here the path forks. Now follow the left-hand path
which shortly comes out above the ravine of Wray Gill. Shortly, it
forks again with the left-hand path dropping down into the bed of the
gill. Follow this path which, after crossing the gill, climbs up to the
right of a scree covered hillock. When it levels out Silver Howe can
be seen ahead, the left-hand and highest point on a hummocky ridge.
Below, to the right, is a boggy basin and beyond that is the craggy
outline of Lang Howe. A cairned and well-worn path leads towards
Silver Howe finishing with a short steep climb.

There is an extensive view down upon Grasmere and Rydal Water,
and towards the south and west. For the descent head westerly (or to
your right as you climbed up to the summit), and down into a hollow
to meet a path which runs across the head of the boggy basin, in the
direction of Lang Howe. Turn right and follow this, passing eventually
to the right of a small tarn choked with plant life. Lang Howe looms
quite impressively ahead. At its foot a cairn will be met and a junction
of paths and to the left another, and slightly larger, tarn will be seen.

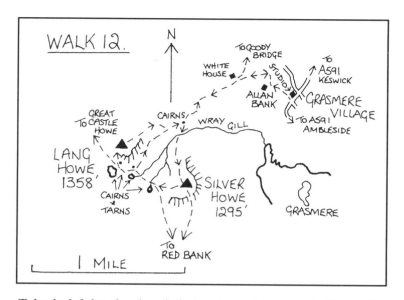

Take the left-hand path and climb up to a saddle graced with a further cairn. Below this will be seen a yet larger plant-choked tarn. The eye will go beyond this however to a superb view of the fells gracing the head of Langdale. Framed between the striking silhouettes of Side Pike and Harrison Stickle are Pike O'Blisco, Crinkle Crags and Bowfell, all displaying their rugged architecture of crag and gill. Now scramble up grass to reach the rounded summit of Lang Howe. The summit has an air of isolation which is remarkable when you consider the popularity of Silver Howe, barely half a mile away, and the network of popular paths surrounding it. It is this charm, combined with its rugged outline from the Silver Howe approach, that gives this walk its higher mountain aspect.

For the descent either return to the second cairn, walk back over the saddle and down to the first cairn, then turn left here and follow the path descending down the left-hand side of the basin under Lang Howe, or follow the crest of Lang Howe for a little way before dropping, right, down grassy slopes to join the same path. This path eventually joins the ascending path on the banks of the Wray Gill. The return to Grasmere village from this point is now simply a reversal of the ascent. 'Howe' or 'how' originally meant a knoll or hillock but was later applied to quite large hills. It sometimes referred to actual or reputed grave mounds.

Walk 13
Medium Walk, 5 miles

Easedale and Codale Tarns

An excellent walk, combining two mountain tarns, an impressive waterfall and an attractive minor summit in its few miles. It can be boggy in places, especially around the tarns, but if only the lower tarn is reached it is still rewarding.

Parking: There is a small car-park next to a housing estate up the Easedale Road. If this is full, however, return and park in Grasmere. Do not park in Easedale Road.

FROM the car-park walk up the lane until, just before an iron gate is reached, a signpost 'Easedale Tarn' will be seen on the left. Go into the trees, cross the footbridge over the stream and pass through a gate on to a stony path. The cascades of Sour Milk Ghyll, which drain from Easedale Tarn, can be seen ahead. The path to them is well-trodden with occasional finger-posts and arrows to assist navigation. It is a pleasant approach, dominated by a circle of craggy hills ranging from Helm Crag on the right to Castle Howe on the left, and with the beck rippling pleasantly below. The path eventually climbs alongside the falls and fine close-ups of the cascades can be seen, particularly if in spate. Above the falls the path levels out and looking back there is a fine view of Seat Sandal and Fairfield. A final gentle climb brings you to the shores of Easedale Tarn. It is an idyllic spot on a calm day, the still dark water reflecting the steep shattered rocks of Tarn Crag. A path encircles the tarn and for those who desire to spend the rest of the day 'festering' there are many excellent spots for picnics, swimming, paddling or sunbathing.

Those however who have energy to spare should continue along the path to the left of the tarn, ignoring a fainter path which forks off even further left towards the shadowy rocks of Blea Rigg Crag. Leaving the tarn behind, the path begins to climb up alongside the feeder stream, under the shadow of the pointed peak of Belles Knott. Eventually a branching path goes right, across the stream. Follow this and a short climb brings you to the shores of Codale Tarn, a smaller tarn and set in more austere surroundings. In mist the next section of the walk could be difficult for the inexperienced and in such circumstances I would advise returning by the way climbed. Under clear skies there is no problem and it offers an interesting route. Follow the path to the northern end of the tarn, where it swings left around the head of the tarn and across the feeder stream. Leave it here, do not cross the stream but follow a fainter path leading

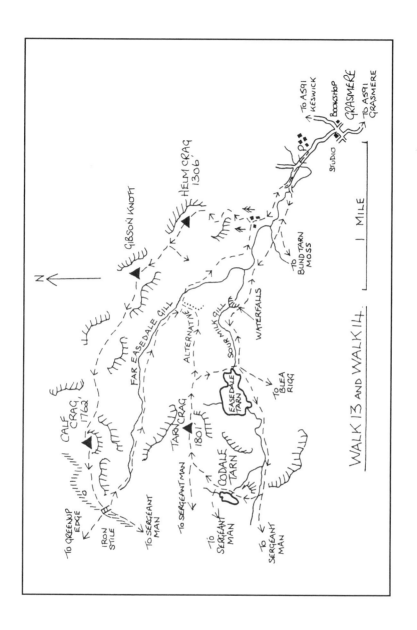

WALK 13 AND WALK 14.

N

To GREENUP EDGE

IRON STILE

CALF CRAG 1762'

To SERGEANT MAN

To SERGEANT MAN

TARN CRAG 1801'

To SERGEANT MAN

CODALE TARN

To SERGEANT MAN

To SERGEANT MAN

EASEDALE TARN

To BLEA RIGG

SOUR MILK GILL

WATERFALLS

ALTERNATIVE

FAR EASEDALE GILL

GIBSON KNOTT

HELM CRAG 1306'

To BUND TARN MOSS

STUDIO

To A591 KESWICK

BOOKSHOP

GRASMERE

To A591 GRASMERE

1 MILE

37

slightly right and heading towards the Tarn Crag ridge ahead. This path crosses over some boggy ground before it begins to climb onto the ridge. The ridge too is somewhat boggy but a path will be met running along it. Turn right along this to reach an obvious gap. The prominent peak on the left of the gap is the summit. Climb up to this for a superb view.

To the south the Langdale Pikes and the Coniston Fells form an impressive skyline. From this angle the latter hills define themselves as individual summits rather than the indistinguishable clump of hills they often appear. Windermere can be seen through the gap of Red Bank and beyond it the distant Pennines with the hump of Ingleborough predominant. Grasmere and Rydal Water glint below and the eye travels north along the grassy ramparts of Fairfield and Helvellyn.

Drop back into the gap and follow the path down on to an undulating grass ridge. Easedale Tarn can now be seen below, to the right. You have a choice of descents now. An obvious path branching down to the right leads back to the shores of Easedale Tarn. The alternative is to continue along the ridge-path which eventually drops down to the left into Far Easedale, joining the last mile or so of Walk 14 near the footbridge over the stream. Either way it is about the same distance to the car-park.

Helm Crag, Calf Crag
and Far Easedale

The ascent of Helm Crag (The Lion and The Lamb), and the exploration of its summit rocks, makes a delightful walk. To continue along the switchback ridge to Calf Crag and to return down Far Easedale simply adds to the pleasure.

Parking: as for Walk 13

WALK up the lane, as before, but this time continue straight ahead passing through the iron-gate. Continue along the road, now unfenced, across a meadow and into a wooded area with private drives leading off. Here the way divides and a signpost indicates 'Helm Crag' to the right. When the walls fall back ignore the old path, which turned right, and follow the new path which climbs past an old quarry and up the fellside in nicely graded curves. It emerges on to the summit ridge just below the 'Lion and the Lamb'. Pause here and enjoy the 'birds-eye' view over the lovely Vale of Grasmere. Turn left and scramble on to the fascinating summit of Helm Crag.

It would appear that in aeons past part of the ridge has collapsed, leaving an undulating crest surmounted by rocky pinnacles which lean slightly over boulder strewn hollows. Exploration of these hollows will reveal several caves amongst the tumbled boulders. The southern-most pinnacle, which forms the figures of 'The Lion and The Lamb' seen from Grasmere village, is given as the summit (1,299 ft) on the one-inch O.S. Map. The highest point however is the airy tip of the northern pinnacle (1,306 ft). This latter pinnacle forms the figures of 'The Old Woman playing an Organ' when viewed from the A591 on the descent from Dunmail Raise. To reach the true summit entails several feet of moderate rock-climbing and care should be taken for it overhangs a considerable drop. This minor fell therefore is one of the handful of summits in Britain in which use of the hands and feet are required to reach it. Given another five hundred to a thousand feet of height it would be regarded as one of the most impressive hills in Britain. 'Helm' is a derivation from an Old Norse word meaning either 'helmet' or 'roofed cattle-shelter'.

Beyond Helm Crag the ridge dips into a grassy saddle and by turning left here a return to the valley can be made if desired. The ridge continues however for a further two miles or so, undulating and curving gradually left to reach its highest point at Calf Crag (1,762 ft). A good path winds pleasantly around or over the many humps. The view ahead is restricted by the bulk of High Raise but across the valley Easedale Tarn can be seen peeping over the Tarn Crag ridge. Below this ridge can be seen the greenish coloured rocks of Deer Bield Crag. Several classic rock-climbs lie on this crag and for a period in the '50s its central buttress was considered 'the last great problem' and many of the famous names of British climbing came to lay siege to it. To your right is the lonely Greenburn valley with the view beyond it blocked by Steel Fell. Probably the best view from this ridge is seen by looking back towards the Vale of Grasmere. My directions could be considered at fault here but in my opinion by having the view at your back it gives you every excuse to pause for a breather.

Beyond Calf Crag, follow the path bearing left, along the rim of the fell, to drop down, alongside old fenceposts, on to the saddle at the head of Far Easedale, which is crowned by a forlorn and somewhat superfluous iron-stile. The right-hand side of the saddle drops into the boggy hollow that drains into Wythburn and a path can be seen running across the back of it and up to the lowest dip in the crest beyond. This dip is Greenup Edge and is a very popular thoroughfare for connecting Grasmere to Borrowdale. To the right of Greenup Edge is the lumpy mass of Ullscarf, whilst to its left, hidden from sight here by steep grass and broken crags, is the plateau of High Raise, or High White Stones as it is sometimes called.

You take the left-hand side of the saddle, following the path down into Far Easedale. It is a pleasant descent though somewhat boggy at times. The path generally follows the stream, one side or the other, which has some fine pools and cascades, and the view towards Grasmere and the hills beyond can be quite beautiful according to the light or the season of the year. The path eventually emerges into the lane initially left. From the iron-stile to the car-park is about three miles.

High Raise and
Sergeant Man

The ascent of High Raise, as described below, is somewhat boggy and .the views restricted. Few Lakeland 2,500 footers however can be climbed less strenuously. This is perhaps the most central of the high fells and the view from its summit, plus the interesting descent over Sergeant Man and the Blea Rigg to Castle How ridge, make the somewhat prosaic climb worthwhile.

Parking: As for Walks 13 and 14.

START as for Walk 14 as far as the turn-off for Helm Crag. Carry straight on here down the lane signposted 'Far Easedale/Greenup Edge'. The stony lane eventually deteriorates into a path which shortly crosses the stream by a footbridge. High on the left can be seen the steep rocks of Deer Bield Crag (described in Walk 14), and on the right is the ridge that forms the major part of that walk. The path climbs gradually, and sometimes boggily, up alongside the stream until a lonely iron-stile is reached on a saddle at the head of the valley. You have now, in effect, reversed the latter section of Walk 14.

The view beyond the saddle is as described in that walk. Follow the path which leads down into the boggy hollow, then across the back of it under the shadow of some broken crags, before climbing up to eventually reach the broad grassy saddle of Greenup Edge. Now the prospect opens up, with Borrowdale lying below and the Buttermere, Newlands and Coledale fells ranked beyond. The remnants of an iron fence, accompanied by a boggy path, will be seen climbing up towards an obvious rocky outcrop on your left. Follow this path to the outcrop and you have virtually finished your climbing for the day. Beyond this outcrop the angle eases as the path leads to more rocks, and all the while the view to the right is opening up. Beyond these rocks the path forks; the left fork follows the fence posts across the grassy plateau whilst that on the right leads gently to the summit cairn and trig point. 'Raise' means 'pile of stones', or 'cairn'.

As previously stated High Raise, or High White Stones as it is sometimes called, is probably the most central of the high fells. The view accordingly is extensive. I do not intend to describe it. Given the right conditions this is the ideal spot for the stranger to Lakeland or the inexperienced walker to spend time over his one-inch O.S. Map and orientate himself. Which peak is which and which hollow hides which lake? It is good fun and the experience gained will be rewarding on future walks.

From the summit a faint path heads south-east; follow this. The featureless grassy plateau that slopes east and south from the summit is unique in an area of craggy peaks. In mist it can be tricky if care is not taken and a compass is far more reliable than the erratic fence posts that cross it. Continuing in this direction the obvious rocky hump of Sergeant Man will soon be seen ahead, marking the edge of the escarpment. 'Man' means a tall cairn, possibly erected by an official. From this summit there is a dramatic view across to the stark profile of Pavey Ark looming over Stickle Tarn and the eye is drawn down the length of Langdale to the yacht-studded waters of Windermere. Turn left from this summit and follow a well-worn path which twists down and around rocky hummocks and generally trends south-east towards the broad ridge dividing Grasmere and Easedale from Langdale.

Soon a path climbing up from the left will be met and Easedale Tarn glimpsed below. If desired a return can be made down this path to the tarn and so back to the car-park. If the weather is fine however it is recommended you continue along the undulating ridge. The path is well cairned and gives impressive views of Harrison Stickle and Pavey Ark, particularly the crags of the latter with the diagonal 'scramble' of Jakes Rake slanting across them. Codale and Easedale tarns can be glimpsed down to the left and Chapel Stile, Elterwater and the Langdale slate-quarries to the right. After crossing Blea Rigg the path drops steeply into a dip. From here a path leads down left to meet Easedale Tarn near its issuing stream. Unless you wish to descend here continue over Great Castle Howe to the next saddle where a fainter path bisects the ridge path.

Turn left down this into a hollow where the path loses itself amongst dwarf-juniper. Keep low down and along the edges of the reed bed (Blind Tarn Moss), and the path will be found again. It descends, swinging right, through thick juniper bushes with a stream rippling unseen below. This section has boggy patches but at a junction of two walls a finger-post points down to the left and a faint path leads down to a gate by the side of a house. Pass through the gate and in front of the house to reach a further gate. Turn left here and two more gates lead to a junction with the path from Easedale Tarn. A sign indicates 'Grasmere' to the right. Turn right and the car-park will soon be reached.

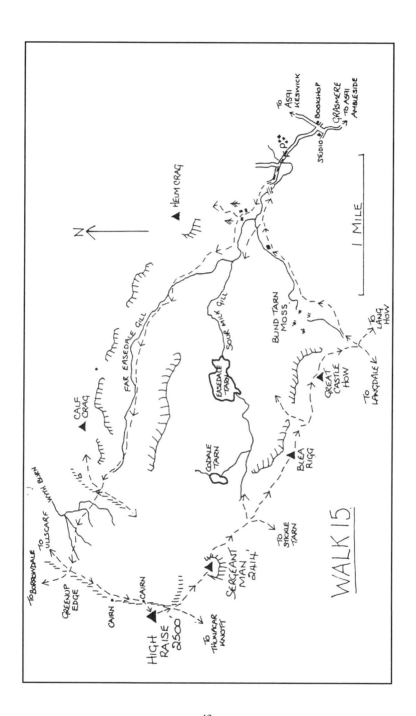

WALK 15

DUNMAIL RAISE

Walk 16   **Fell Walk, 6 miles**

Fairfield and Seat Sandal

The most popular way to climb Fairfield is by way of the Fairfield Horseshoe. The walk described below is a less well-known and shorter route but nevertheless gives interesting views and also includes the ascent of one of Lakeland's lesser known fells.

Parking: In the lay-by, near the Dunmail Field Centre, formerly the Achille Ratti Climbing Club hut, on the east side of Dunmail Raise (GR 329111).

CLIMB over either of two stiles and walk diagonally left to the foot of Raise Beck. A good path now follows the right-hand bank of the beck. It is steep and rocky at first but eventually the angle eases although the ground becomes boggier. Looking back and down, the huge cairn marking the crest of Dunmail Raise can be seen. This is reputedly the site of a battle in which the Britons of Cumbria, under their King Dunmail, were defeated by the Saxons. Steel Fell blocks all view across the Raise until some height is gained and then the western fells start to thrust into view.

When the saddle is eventually reached the waters of Grisedale Tarn can be seen below. Legend also has it that the survivors of the battle fled up Raise Beck and upon reaching the tarn threw their dead king's crown into its dark waters, and that their ghosts are reputed to repeat the performance annually. Such legends make interesting and delightful reading but there is also some hard evidence that King Dunmail died peacefully in his bed, in Rome, many years after the reputed battle.

To the left of the tarn rises the grassy bulk of Dollywaggon Pike. Beyond the tarn the ground drops away into Grisedale and rising out of this valley can be seen the rounded summit of St. Sunday Crag, its northern slope surmounted by a belt of steep crags. From St. Sunday Crag the skyline dips into the gap of Deepdale Hause before rising again over the rocky hump of Cofa Pike and then steeper still up to the broad summit of Fairfield. 'The light-coloured or mottled peak', your objective. To reach this, start by turning right and following the path that leads around the tarn and into the gap dividing Fairfield from Seat Sandal, the fell on your immediate right. This gap is called Grisedale Hause, 'hause' meaning 'a pass', and upon reaching it turn left and begin the climb up the path running alongside a tumbled

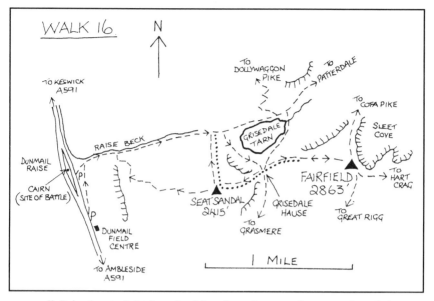

wall. It is about eight-hundred feet from here to the summit and the first few hundred are fairly steep but eventually the angle eases and the summit plateau and cairn are reached. The summit of Fairfield is a broad plateau and in misty or winter conditions care should be taken. The eastern edge is rimmed with steep crags which accumulate snow cornices and there have been fatal accidents here. The views are extensive. Windermere can be seen to the south, and to the east the eye drops into the lonely depths of Sleet Cove before rising to the long barrier of the High Street fells, to the left of which, on a clear day, Cross Fell may be seen above the Eden valley. To the north the 'coves' and 'edges' of Helvellyn can be seen in superb detail. Striding Edge is the long ridge nearest to us with Swirrel Edge and the shapely cone of Catsycam beyond. To the west the fells stretch from Coniston Old Man to Grisedale Pike, with the dome-like shape of Great Gable particularly predominant.

Return to Grisedale Hause by the same path but then follow the wall climbing steeply up the opposite slope. A short steep pull soon eases out on to the grassy summit of Seat Sandal, 'Sandal's shieling', which you will more than likely have to yourself. There is a fine view down into the Vale of Grasmere. Raise Beck can be easily reached by following the northerly heading wall, but a more interesting alternative is to head westerly down easy-angled grass slopes. There is no path but the ground is easy and as height is lost you are rewarded by a fine and unusual view, to the right, along the river-like length of

Thirlmere towards distant Skiddaw. When the ground begins to steepen gradually work right and a faint path can be found which leads down to the mouth of the valley of the Raise Beck and a junction with the initial ascending path.